OCRAFTS

Dream
edroom

ECOCRAFTS

Dream
Bedroom

KINGFISHER

KINGFISHER

Kingfisher Publications Plc
New Penderel House
283–288 High Holborn
London WC1V 7HZ
www.kingfisherpub.com

First published by Kingfisher Publications Plc 2007
2 4 6 8 10 9 7 5 3 1
1TR/0107/C&C/MAR(MAR)/128OJIEX-GREEN/C

Author: Rebecca Craig

For Toucan
Editor: Theresa Bebbington
Design: Leah Germann
Additional Makes by: Dawn Brend,
Melanie Williams, Kirsty Neale
Photography Art Direction: Jane Thomas
Editorial Assistant: Hannah Bowen
Photographer: Andy Crawford
Editorial Director: Ellen Dupont

For Kingfisher
Editorial Manager: Russell Mclean
Art Director: Mike Davis
Senior Production Controller: Lindsey Scott
DTP Coordinator: Catherine Hibbert

A CIP catalogue record for this book
is available from the British Library.

ISBN 978 07534 1452 1

Printed in China

**The paper used for the cover and text pages is
made from 100% recycled post consumer waste.**

Contents

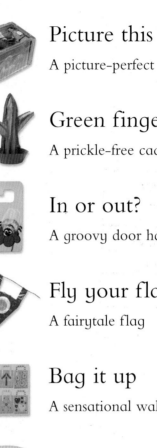

Eco-wise

Turn your bedroom into your own, unique space by decorating it with things you have made yourself. These items will make your room a fun place to be. And they will be special to you – no one else will have things that are exactly the same as yours.

As well as being really special, all the projects in this book help the environment by using everyday objects found in your home. A lot of them are things you would have thrown away. Inside you'll find ways to use an old cardboard box and tubes to make a desk tidy, CD cases to create a picture frame for photos,

plastic bags to make flags, and even comics to make a stool. Recycling helps the planet because it reuses things that would have ended up in the trash.

Around the world, tonnes of rubbish end up in landfills each year. In fact, in 1999 the

3 'R's to recycling

About half of the rubbish in our dustbins can be recycled. Follow these steps to help prevent rubbish being sent to landfills or incinerators.

REDUCE – Encourage your parents to buy products that have little or no packaging.

REUSE – Find new ways to use jars, tins, plastic containers and other durable things.

RECYCLE – If you can't reuse something but it can be recycled, help your parents recycle it.

Fresh Kills landfill in New York City became the largest man-made structure in the world, overtaking the Great Wall of China. Because air and water cannot reach the rubbish buried deep in the landfill, the rubbish does not decompose, or break down. Even after 30 years you can still read newspapers buried in a landfill!

Sometimes rubbish goes to an incinerator, where it is burned. But this isn't a good solution either. The ashes still have to be disposed of – and they can be toxic. Burning rubbish also creates air pollution. The only really good way to reduce waste is to recycle. For example, by recycling plastic, 50 per cent less energy is used than if it was burned in an incinerator. And the plastic is used to make something else, such as a fleece jacket or even a park bench.

What you can do

Bored of an old toy? Try swapping it with a good friend for another toy. Both you and your friend will be recycling toys.

Look for toys in boot sales and charity shops. This way you'll be helping to reuse things that would otherwise go to a landfill. And they probably won't come with the packaging that protects new toys.

Bring your old clothes to a charity shop so they can be reused by someone else.

If you have old books that are now too easy for you, give them to younger friends who will still find them difficult to read.

Pass on old CDs that you no longer like to friends and family who might enjoy listening to them.

ruler

scissors

pen

pencil

paintbrush

tape

paint

PVA glue

Getting started

Before starting a project, make sure you have everything you need. If you don't know how to trace a picture or make papier-mâché, follow the steps here. Some craft supplies are not meant for children under 13 to use. If you're not sure if something is safe to use, ask an adult if it's okay. When using craft supplies that have a strong odour, work in a room that has plenty of fresh air. If an object is difficult to cut, ask an adult to help.

TRACING A PICTURE

If you have a pencil, pen, tracing paper and tape, you can copy any picture you want. The pencil should have soft lead – this will make it easier to do the rubbing over the back. Use a pen with a hard point to make the lines really crisp.

STEP 1

Tape down a sheet of tracing paper over the picture you wish to draw. Using a pen with a hard point, copy the picture onto the tracing paper.

STEP 2

Remove the tracing paper from the picture. Rub a soft-lead pencil on the back of the tracing paper where you can see the lines you have drawn.

STEP 3

Tape the paper onto the object where you want the picture. Draw over the lines in pen. Remove the tracing paper. The design will be on the object.

MAKING PAPIER-MÂCHÉ

By soaking newspaper in a paste made from flour and water, you can mould and build up many shapes. Use long strips of newspaper when you need to add strength.

The smaller pieces of newspaper are easier for moulding. Build up layers until you have the shape you want. Let the paper dry completely before decorating it.

STEP 1

Measure out one part of flour to about two parts of water. For example, use 125 grams of flour and 450 millilitres of water. Mix 4 tablespoons of salt with the flour to prevent the papier-mâché going mouldy.

STEP 2

Pour the water over the flour. Mix with a wooden spoon until you have a smooth paste without lumps – it should look like thick glue. If it is too thick, add a little more water. If it is too thin, add some more flour.

STEP 3

Rip up some newspaper into chunks or strips, following the steps for your project. Dip a chunk or strip of newspaper into the paste until it is really soaked. It is now ready to use.

Piggy pennies

You can turn a plastic bottle into a really cool piggy bank that will make a great gift for saving coins. The upside-down squeezable ketchup bottles work best.

YOU WILL NEED:

squeezable plastic bottle, scissors, pink paint, paintbrush, bottle corks, black felt-tip pen, PVA glue, pink pipe cleaner, pencil, pink foam or felt, googly eyes

STEP 1

Make sure you wash out the insides of the bottle and cap completely. Scrub off the label after letting the bottle soak in water. Allow to dry thoroughly.

STEP 2

Ask an adult to puncture a hole in the middle of the bottle with scissors, then to cut a slot large enough for coins. The cut should be smooth, with no sharp edges.

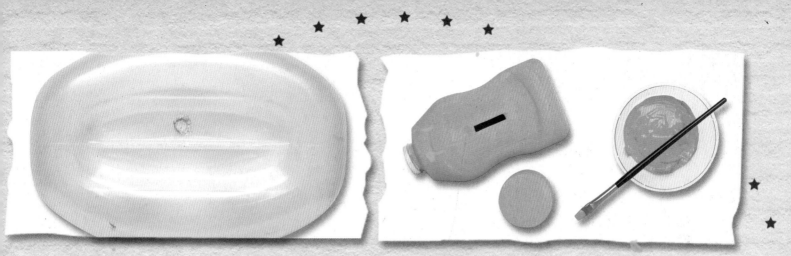

STEP 3

Ask an adult to also make a small hole at the base of the bottle, using scissors.

STEP 4

Paint both the bottle and the bottle cap a bright pink colour. Let the paint dry.

STEP 5

If you want short, stubby legs, ask an adult to cut two bottle corks in half. Paint the bottle corks bright pink. Let the paint dry completely.

STEP 6

Using a black felt-tip pen, carefully draw an outline on each cork for the pig's hoofs, then fill in the outline.

Piggy pennies

STEP 7

Screw the cap back onto the bottle. Glue the cork legs to the bottom of the bottle.

STEP 8

To make a curly tail, wrap a piece of pipe cleaner around a pencil.

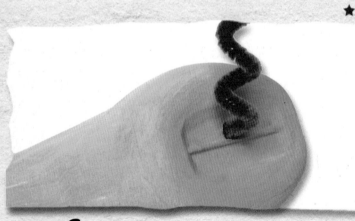

STEP 9

Bend a small hook at the end of the tail (it will help the tail stay in place). Poke the hooked end into the hole in the base of the bottle.

STEP 10

Using a pair of scissors, cut out two ears from a piece of pink felt or foam.

STEP 11

Glue the ears to the sides of your pig. Try to keep them the same spacing from the centre.

STEP 12

Use the felt-tip pen to outline and fill in the pig's nostrils. Then glue a pair of googly eyes onto the pig (or draw them in with the pen).

Try changing the ears, tail and paint colour to make a cow or sheep.

Once this piggy bank is full, take off the cap and spend your savings. Then you can use the bank to start saving money again!

Funky files

This folder holder is the perfect item for storing your magazines, comics or homework. You can make it with an old cereal box and some wrapping paper.

YOU WILL NEED:
cereal box, ruler, pen, scissors, paint, paintbrush, wrapping paper, PVA glue

STEP
On the front of the cereal box, draw a line from the top corner to the other edge, halfway down. Repeat on the back, then add a line across the side to join the two lines. Cut along these lines to remove the top part of the box.

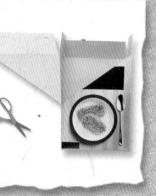

STEP 2
Paint the inside of your box a bright colour. Allow the paint to dry.

STEP 3
Cut a piece of wrapping paper about 5 centimetres longer and wider than the bottom, back and front of the box.

STEP 4

Glue the long piece of wrapping paper to the box. Fold the edges up at the sides and tuck in the corners neatly.

STEP 5

For the sides, lie the box down on some more paper. Draw a line at the same angle as the top of the box. Repeat with the other side. Cut the paper.

STEP 6

Centre the box on the paper and crease the bottom edges of the paper where it will fold, for a neat finish. Spread glue on one side of the box and lie it down. Then glue the bottom and the other side.

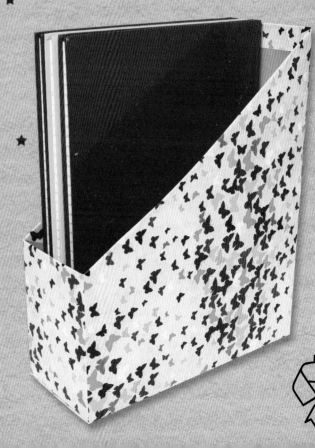

STEP 7

For a neat finish at the top of the box, cut a small notch at each corner to turn down the paper. Glue and press the edges down.

15

Handy holder

You can make a crafty jewellery holder in the shape of your own hand from papier-mâché! Or make a spooky skeleton hand by painting the hand black and adding some white bones.

YOU WILL NEED:

old cardboard, pen, bowl, scissors, tape, flour and water paste, newspaper, paint, paintbrush, glittery shapes (optional), PVA glue

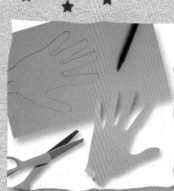

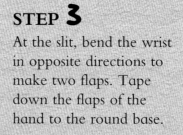

STEP 1

Place the bowl on the cardboard. Draw round it to make a perfect circle, then cut out the circle. This will be the base.

STEP 2

Draw round your hand, making sure you include some of your wrist. Cut out the hand, then cut a slit a few centimetres up the middle of the wrist.

STEP 3

At the slit, bend the wrist in opposite directions to make two flaps. Tape down the flaps of the hand to the round base.

STEP 4

Mix up a flour and water paste (see page 9). Then cut newspaper into strips about the width of your finger and about 20 centimetres long.

STEP 5

Soak the strips in the paste. Smooth the strips over the hand and base, making sure to cover them completely.

STEP 6

Scrunch up a sheet of newspaper into a sausage shape and dip it in the paste. Place a sausage on each finger to add bulk. Cover the sausages with strips of newspaper.

STEP 7

Once the newspaper is completely dry, paint over the hand with a solid colour. You may need to paint it again to make the colour really strong.

STEP 8

Once the paint is dry, use white and pink paint to make fingernails. When the paint is dry, cover the hand in PVA glue and, if you want, add some glittery shapes.

Once the glue is dry, your handy holder will be ready for some shiny rings and bracelets.

Alien attack

With a few sturdy paper plates (plastic-coated ones are best) and a plastic bowl, you can make your own space station. Before you use them, make sure the plates and bowl are completely clean and dry.

YOU WILL NEED:

plastic bowl, paper towel, two paper plates, pencil or pen, scissors, string, tape, spray paint, scrap cardboard, foil, tracing paper, PVA glue, thin cardboard, coloured pencils or crayons (or paint and a paintbrush), paperclip

STEP 1

Use a pencil or pen to make a hole in the centre of the bowl. First place a wad of paper towel under the bowl to absorb the shock, and punch a hole with the pencil.

STEP 2

To hang your space station, cut a length of string and poke it through the hole in the bowl.

18

STEP 3

Tie a knot in the string, such as a figure-of-eight, to keep the string from slipping out of the hole.

STEP 4

Tape the two paper plates together around the edges. They will become the rim of the space station.

STEP 5

Centre the bowl, upside down, over the top of the paper plates. The string should be coming out from the top of the bowl. Tape the bowl to the plates.

STEP 6

Ask an adult to spray paint the space station for you, using a piece of cardboard in front of the string to keep paint off it. Hang up the station to let it dry.

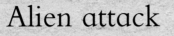

Alien attack

STEP 7

Cut out small circles of foil. These will become the windows of the space station. Glue the foil circles, evenly spaced, around the bowl.

STEP 8

To make the alien, trace the template (see page 46) onto tracing paper. Transfer the alien to a piece of thin cardboard (see page 8).

STEP 9

Colour in your alien, using coloured pencils or crayons, or paint it. Use as many colours as you wish.

STEP 10

Once the alien is decorated (and any paint is dry), cut it out. A simple shape is fine. (If you are really good at using scissors, you can cut closer round the alien.)

STEP 11

Tape a paperclip to the back of the alien. Then slip the paperclip onto the string of your space station.

Hang your space station in your room, using the string. If you want, try making another space station using a plastic container, such as a yogurt pot, and make the windows using caps from bottles.

You can slide your alien up and down on the string whenever you want.

Buried treasure

Make a treasure chest to store all your favourite secret trinkets! You will need a cardboard box, such as a shoebox. One without an attached top is best, so you won't have to remove it.

YOU WILL NEED:

cardboard box, cardboard, felt-tip pen, scissors, card, masking tape, newspaper, flour and water paste, sandpaper, paint, paintbrush, garden wire or string, ribbon, sweet wrappers, PVA glue

STEP 1

To make a lid for the chest, place the box on a larger piece of cardboard and trace round it. Cut carefully along the outline, making sure you have straight edges.

STEP 2

Cut a piece of card the same length as the 'lid' in step 1, but make it 5 centimetres wider.

STEP 3

Tape the card onto the cardboard lid along one side only.

STEP 4

Gently bend over the card to make an arch, then tape the other side to the cardboard.

STEP 5

To make the end sections, stand your lid on some card and trace round the ends of the lid.

STEP 6

Carefully cut out the two end sections.

STEP 7

Now tape the two end sections to your lid. Don't worry if there are gaps, as these will be covered.

STEP 8

Make a flour and water paste (see page 9) and cut up some strips of newspaper. Soak the newspaper in the paste and cover the box and lid with a layer of newspaper. Allow the newspaper to dry.

STEP 9

Using fine sandpaper, gently rub down your box and lid. This will give the box a textured finish.

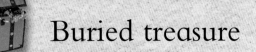

Buried treasure

STEP 10

Paint the outside of your box and lid a solid colour, such as gold or a bright colour. Allow the paint to dry, then paint the inside of the box a contrasting colour, such as red.

STEP 11

Paint an edge round the box, two stripes and rectangles on the ends for the handles. Paint a framed edge and stripes on the lid. Once dry, make 'studs' with a black pen.

STEP 12

Ask an adult to make two holes for each handle. Form a 'C' shape out of garden wire, bend the ends and poke them into the holes. Push the ends down; cover with tape.

STEP 13

Place the lid on the box. Cut two pieces of ribbon, the same colour as your stripes, about 10 centimetres long. Glue these over the stripes, centred between the lid and box. These will act as hinges for your lid.

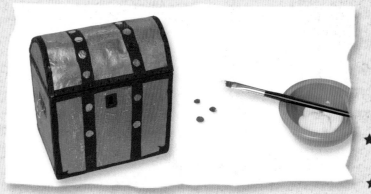

STEP 14

Cut out round-shaped 'jewels' from some colourful sweet wrappers.

STEP 15

Glue the jewels along the stripes. For the final touch, paint a rectangle on the box where you would like a keyhole. Once the paint is dry, use a felt-tip pen to draw a keyhole.

This treasure chest is great for storing real treasure, such as your favourite jewellery.

Instead of wire, you can use string for the handles.

In the jungle

A cardboard box, some kitchen rolls and a jar lid can be turned into an exotic jungle desk tidy. It's ideal for holding all of your pens, pencils and paperclips.

YOU WILL NEED:

cardboard box, felt-tip pen, scissors, paintbrush, paint, cardboard tubes (from kitchen roll or wrapping paper), jar lid, coloured paper, tissue paper, PVA glue

ECOFACT

Cardboard can be recycled four or five times before its fibres become too short to be used again. Recycled cardboard can be used to make more boxes and packaging, and it can also be turned into stationery and animal bedding.

STEP 1

Cut out the corner of a cardboard box. Draw the outline of some bushes and a palm tree. You can follow the lines in the picture above – they don't need to be exact.

STEP 2

Cut round your outline, using a pair of scissors. Be careful when cutting into the corners.

STEP 3

Paint the base colour of the grass, leaves and tree, using different shades of green and some brown. Let the paint dry completely.

STEP 4

Add details to your tree, painting in the branches. Then add details to the grass and bushes. You can paint in a tiger or other animal if you wish.

STEP 5

Cut the cardboard tube into different lengths. Paint them a bright colour inside and green on the outside. Then paint the inside of a jar lid and its rim green. Allow the paint to dry.

STEP 6

Paint some tall leaves onto the tubes, along with some flowers. You can paint eyes for an animal hiding behind some of the leaves.

In the jungle

STEP 7

Draw the outline of a parrot onto a piece of cardboard left over from your box. You can follow the outline used in the picture above. Don't worry if it is not exactly the same. Cut out the parrot along your outline.

STEP 8

Paint in the parrot, using one colour at a time. Make sure the paint is dry before adding another colour. Once the paint is dry, use a black felt-tip pen to draw an eye.

STEP 9

Cut out several flowers from coloured paper. You can use three or four different colours to make your desk tidy really colourful.

STEP 10

Scrunch up some little balls of tissue paper and glue them to the centre of the flowers. Let the glue dry, then glue your flowers to the base of the desk tidy – make sure they won't be in the way of the tubes and lid.

Arrange all your pieces before you glue them in place, to make sure you like the way they look.

As a final step, glue the parrot onto a leaf of the palm tree and the cardboard tubes and jar lid to the base. Your desk tidy is now ready to be filled.

Picture this

Make a display cube out of old CD cases to show off your fabulous photos or pictures. You'll be able to frame five of your favourites at the same time.

YOU WILL NEED:
••
five CD cases, styrofoam packaging, pen, scissors, photographs or pictures, ruler, glue, paintbrush

STEP 1
You need only the clear outer part of the CD cases, so take them apart – but avoid cracking them.

STEP 2
Trace round one case onto a thin piece of styrofoam packaging and cut it out with scissors.

STEP 3
Cut a second piece of styrofoam as in step 2. Glue the two pieces together, one exactly on top of the other.

STEP 4
Cut and glue together several pieces of styrofoam until you have a block that is the same height as the CD case.

STEP 5

Measure the case with a ruler and cut a photo to the same size. Test the fit of the photo in the case.

STEP 6

Draw round the first photo onto the back of the other photos. Cut the photos with scissors.

STEP 7

Glue the CD cases to the sides and top of the styrofoam cube. Allow the glue to dry.

STEP 8

Once the glue is dry, you can slip a photo into each CD case.

If you get bored of a photo, use the gap at the end of the CD case to take it out and replace it with a new favourite.

You can try filling the CDs with dried leaves or pressed flowers.

Green fingers

You can make your own cactus with old cardboard tubes and a plastic container. This cactus does not need watering – and it won't have thorns to prick you!

YOU WILL NEED:
....
plastic bowl or container, paint, paintbrush, two cardboard tubes (from kitchen roll or wrapping paper), scissors, tape, flour and water paste, newspaper

STEP 1
To make the flowerpot, cut the rim off your bowl if it has one.

STEP 2
Cut a cardboard tube into two pieces, with one section a little longer than the other.

STEP 3
Cut the two pieces diagonally at the top. This will allow you to attach the 'arms' of the cactus at an angle. Save a left-over piece.

STEP 4
Tape another cardboard tube into the bowl and add the left-over piece to the top. Tape the 'arms' onto the body of the cactus at an angle.

STEP 5

Mix up a flour and water paste (see page 9) and tear up strips and chunks of newspaper. Soak the paper in the paste, and start covering the tubes.

STEP 6

To make spines on your cactus, scrunch up a sheet of newspaper into a long shape. Paste it to the side of the cactus. Repeat three or four times.

STEP 7

Paint a coat of paint on the cactus and pot. You might need a few coats so the newspaper does not show through. Let the paint dry between coats.

STEP 8

Once the last coat of paint is dry, mix up a darker colour and carefully paint the spines to make them stand out.

You can also use a real flowerpot to show off your cool cactus.

33

In or out?

You can make your own personal door hanger from a cereal box to tell people when you are in your bedroom and when you have gone out.

YOU WILL NEED:
....
tracing paper, pen, pencil, thin cardboard, scissors, paint, paintbrushes, plastic bottle, PVA glue, googly eyes

STEP 1

Use the template (see page 47) to trace the shape of the door hanger. Transfer the outline to a piece of thin cardboard (see page 8).

STEP 2

Using a pair of scissors, cut out the door hanger. Try to cut it out as smoothly as you can.

STEP 3

Carefully draw a simple flower at the bottom of the hanger. Start with the circle in the centre, then draw one petal at a time. Finish off with the stem.

STEP 4

Paint the background colour around the flower. Allow the paint to dry.

STEP 5

Paint the flower. A bright colour such as red will make the petals really stand out. Don't forget to paint the centre of the flower and the stem. Let the paint dry.

STEP 6

Trace the bumblebee from the template (see page 46). Transfer the tracing to a piece of thin cardboard and cut out the outline of the bee.

In or out?

STEP 7

Colour in the black areas of the bee: the stripes, the legs and the head. Don't paint in the eyes, so you will know where to glue them on later. Let the paint dry.

STEP 8

Paint the yellow stripes. While the paint is wet, use a thin paintbrush to make streaks so that the bee looks fuzzy.

STEP 9

When the paint is dry, glue the bee to the flower. Cut out two wings from a plastic bottle. Glue them to the bee.

STEP 10

As a final touch, glue a pair of googly eyes to your bumblebee.

Paint a flying bee on the other side of the hanger, then write a different message on each side. Use one message to let your family know when you are in, and the other to say you have gone out.

Buzzed off!

Bee-ing in!

37

Fly your flag

You can turn your bed into a fairytale palace or a castle for knights by decorating it with these flags made from plastic shopping bags.

YOU WILL NEED:
....
plastic shopping bags, tape, scissors, pen, two bowls, ruler, straws

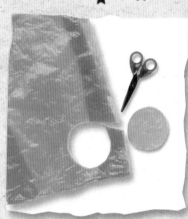

STEP 1
To make a triangle, fold over the top corner on the handle-free end of a plastic bag. Tape it down.

STEP 2
Fold over the other side of the bag to form a point in the centre of the bag. Tape it down.

STEP 3
Using a bag that is a different colour, draw round a bowl to make a circle. Cut it out.

STEP 4
Draw round a smaller bowl onto a bag that is a third colour, then cut it out.

38

STEP 5

Tape the circle shapes onto the triangle-shaped base of the flag.

STEP 6

Cut out a strip from a bag. Lay it across the flag. Use a ruler and pen to mark the ends, then cut them.

STEP 7

Tape the strip to the flag. Repeat steps 6 and 7 until you have as many strips as you want.

STEP 8

Tape two straws together and thread them through the handles of your flag.

STEP 9

Tape the handles onto the straws. Your flag is ready for flying.

Attach a stick to the straws to make your flag fly higher.

To make bunting for your bedroom, you can make several flags and thread them onto string instead of the straws.

Bag it up

Why not try making a cheerful wall tidy from some clean takeaway bags? It will be ideal for storing small toys, hair clips and scrunchies, or even some letter-writing supplies.

ECOFACT
Making paper bags creates 70 per cent more air pollution and 50 times more water pollution than making plastic bags. Recycling paper bags also requires more energy than the energy needed to recycle plastic bags.

YOU WILL NEED:
paper bags, sturdy cardboard, craft paper, scissors, PVA glue, paintbrush, pen, small bowl, large bowl or plate, coin, fake jewels, paint, piece of string, strong tape

STEP 1
Decide how many bags you want for your wall tidy. Choose a piece of sturdy cardboard that will be large enough to hold them all.

STEP 2
Spread some glue over the back of a sheet of craft paper cut to the same size as the sturdy cardboard. Glue the paper to the cardboard, smoothing out any bubbles.

STEP **3**

Use a bowl to draw three circles on a piece of craft paper. Cut these out with a pair of scissors.

STEP **4**

Make larger circles on a different coloured paper by using a larger bowl or plate, and smaller circles on a third colour by using a large coin. Cut these out with a pair of scissors.

STEP **5**

Glue the circles together, with the largest on the bottom and the smallest on top. Glue the circles onto a takeaway bag.

Bag it up

STEP 6

Glue some jewels along the handle and on the small paper circles. Decorate the other bags with pieces of coloured paper cut into different shapes, such as hearts, moons and butterflies. Or paint on a pattern, such as an arrow or a flower. Glue jewels on them too.

STEP 7

Spread dabs of glue on the back of one bag. Press it down on top of the cardboard backing.

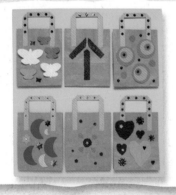

STEP 8

Continue gluing the bags to the cardboad backing until they are all in place.

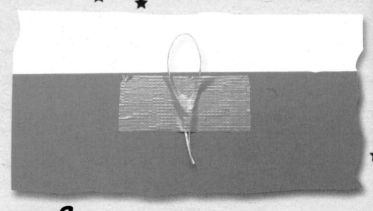

STEP 9

Cut a piece of string and form a loop. Tape it to the back of the cardboard with strong tape. Make sure the loop is centred along the top edge of the backing.

Your wall tidy is ready to be hung on the wall and filled. If you want to put heavier items in the bags, tape extra loops at the top corners of the wall tidy.

43

Take a seat

You can turn old comics, magazines or newspapers into a cool stool. You'll need about 40 of these, as well as a large container to use as a mould.

YOU WILL NEED:

comics or magazines, elastic bands or string, large saucepan or container, old belt, cardboard, pen, scissors, old top or other clothing, dressmaker's pencil, tape, PVA glue

STEP 1
Roll up each comic neatly and fasten it with an elastic band or string.

STEP 2
Place your rolled-up comics inside a large saucepan or container, one by one.

STEP 3
Continue filling up the saucepan or container until it is full. Make sure the tops of the comics are at the same height.

STEP 4
Fasten an old belt around the comics, then remove them from the saucepan. If necessary, slide the belt down to the centre of the comics, then tighten it.

STEP 5

Place the comics over a piece of cardboard. Draw a circle round them, then cut out the circle with a pair of scissors.

STEP 6

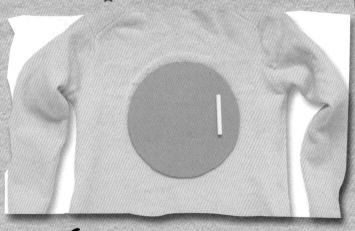

Place the cardboard circle on an old piece of clothing and draw round it, using a dressmaker's pencil. Cut out a circle 2.5 centimetres larger all around.

STEP 7

Place the cardboard circle in the centre of the fabric circle. Cut notches every 5 centimetres and tape the flaps down.

Glue the fabric-covered circle onto the top of the comics. It will make a comfortable seat for your stool.

This makes a great stool or footrest for you or your friends.

Alien template
(for pages 18–21)

Bee template
(for pages 34–37)

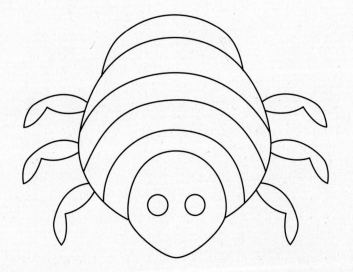

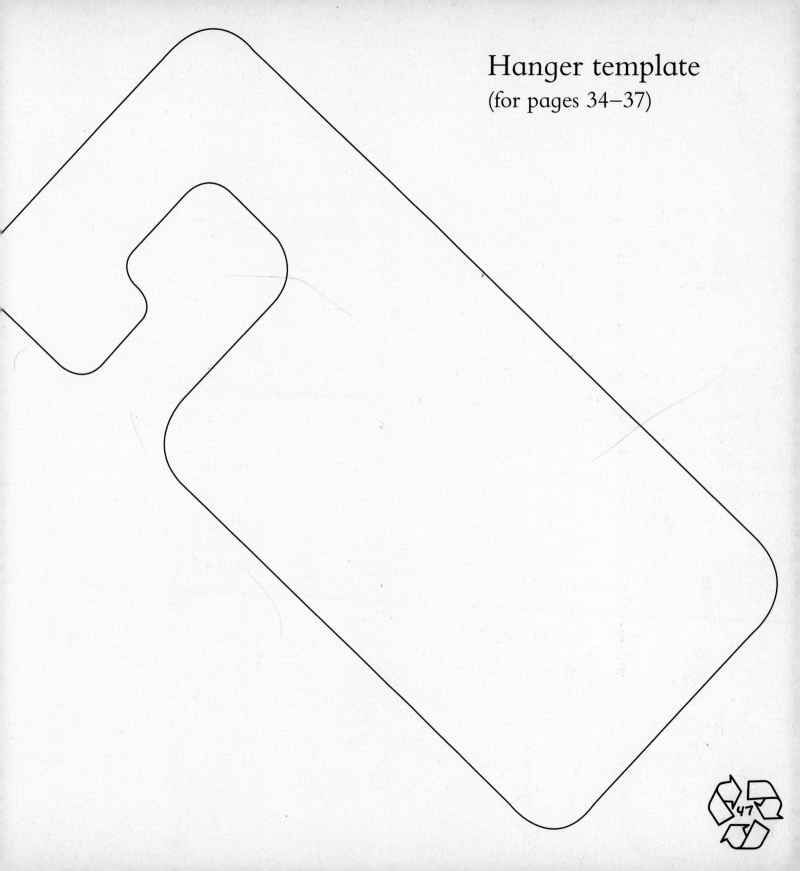

Hanger template
(for pages 34–37)

47

Index